Original title:
Chains of Memory

Copyright © 2025 Creative Arts Management OÜ
All rights reserved.

Author: Sophia Kingsley
ISBN HARDBACK: 978-1-80586-002-0
ISBN PAPERBACK: 978-1-80586-474-5

The Gravity of Reflection

In the mirror, I spot my sock,
Blue with polka dots—what a shock!
It seems it lost its partner fair,
A tale of laundry gone to where?

My thoughts float back, like feathers blown,
To days of smiles and all I've known.
A jumble of laughs, that's the key,
To lighten the burden of memory.

Anchored in Echoes

Bouncing voices in my head,
Recalling where my old shoes led.
One's laced with wisdom, one with flair,
Each step we took—oh, life's a dare!

Laughter ricochets off the wall,
While echoes of my blunders call.
"Did you really wear that at prom?"
My brain's a circus, and I'm the clown.

Faded Photographs of the Heart

Old photos tucked in dusty drawers,
Each snapshot whispers tales galore.
I dance with grannies in their prime,
And don't forget that fish—what a slime!

A laugh, a smile, a silly face,
In every click, there's love and grace.
Yet one thing's clear, beyond the jest,
Who put the cake on Auntie's chest?

Relics of a Silent Past

Old toys sit quiet, watching me,
Dusty relics from my jubilee.
A broken robot, a doll with flair,
"I swear I fed you!" floats in the air.

Memories stacked like old board games,
Each piece connects with quirky claims.
Yet here I stand, half lost, half found,
In laughter's grip, I'm glory-bound.

Time's Embrace

Ticking clocks and wafting dreams,
Old socks lost in time's weird schemes.
A dance of dust on forgotten shelves,
Waving at shadows, we laugh ourselves.

Each quirky photo, a snapshot tease,
Reminds me I once had crazy knees.
Muffled giggles, the past does prance,
In this bewildering, silly dance.

A Garden of Lost Stories

Weeds of wisdom sprout and grow,
In corners where wild stories flow.
Each petal whispers a secret tale,
Of mishaps, laughs, and a dog named Gale.

Sunlight tickles forgotten songs,
As paper boats sail where they don't belong.
Wandering paths with a twisty grin,
In the garden of laughter, let the fun begin!

Shattered Reflections

Mirrors crack with laughter lines,
Echoes of mischief in dashed designs.
Each shard tells stories, wild and strange,
Of hairdos fluffed and pants that change.

Glimpses of me, quite unsure,
Winking back with a playful blur.
In every fracture, a chuckle finds,
The funny twists of our tangled minds.

The Tangle of Thoughts

Balloons of ideas float in the air,
Tangled up with a twist of hair.
Jokes and jumbles spin 'round my head,
As I search for the meaning of what she said.

Coffee spills, but laughter pours,
As thoughts collide like runaway doors.
With a wink and a nod, we set it free,
In this carnival of chaos, just you and me.

Threads of Forgotten Dreams

In a closet of wishes, I found a sock,
With a story of laughter, it seems quite the shock.
It danced with old dust bunnies, a wild little crew,
Sipping tea with lost socks, in a world that once grew.

A hat with a feather, it wanted to sing,
About moments of nonsense, and foolish old things.
It twirled in the sunlight, like a bird with a flair,
Chasing echoes of giggles that drifted in air.

Unraveling Time's Tapestry

In my attic I stumbled upon a strange quilt,
Each patch told a story, or so it was built.
One corner had dancing, a ball in full swing,
While another was napping, missing out on the bling.

A pillow that whispered of dreams long held tight,
Claiming it saw a bear in my dreams just last night.
A patch of bright colors, so vibrant and bold,
Spilled secrets of life, or maybe just gold.

Remnants of a Faded Yesterday

I found an old sandwich, tucked under a bed,
It smiled at me kindly, though old and quite spread.
With pickles and mustard, a weird combination,
It laughed as it shared, its own celebration.

Next to it lay a shoe, with stories to tell,
Of dances and missteps, and mishaps as well.
Worn soles, but still tapping, with rhythm and cheer,
It sang of the jigs that were lost to the year.

Ghosts of Moments Lost

In a corner of my mind, a ghost wore a hat,
Thinking of mischief while chasing a stray cat.
It reminded me softly of pies made with fluff,
And how laughter can linger, even when times are tough.

A memory stumbled, quite tipsy and bright,
Waving a wand, casting shadows of light.
"Remember that party?" it exclaimed with a grin,
"Where the punch got too wobbly, spilling all over the din!"

Labyrinths of the Mind

In the attic of my brain, things pile high,
Forgotten socks and a pet tarantula, oh my!
Recipes for soup, scribbled on old socks,
A map to treasure, if I only had some clocks.

Cats dancing salsa, on a Tuesday night,
Kittens hold board meetings, oh what a sight!
Echoes of laughter, misplaced and absurd,
Chasing those memories, they fly like a bird.

Stairways to Oblivion

In a world where fish wear hats, life is sweet,
I forgot my grocery list, now I just eat beet.
Every step I take is a trip down the lane,
Where I meet my old shoes, that drive me insane.

Cupcakes that sing, to the tune of the rain,
Ordinary spoons that can never complain.
Lost in a world where the clocks just refuse,
To tell me the time, I just waltz in my shoes.

The Mosaic of Remembrance

My childhood painted with crayons and glue,
Dancing on rooftops, just me and my shoe.
Piecing together the past so surreal,
Each fragment of laughter, with a side of meal.

Bananas in pajamas, join me for tea,
Talking to chairs, how absurd it can be!
With every recall, a giggle or sigh,
Waltzing through moments, that just dance on by.

Unraveled Threads of Time

In a cupboard where socks have all run away,
I find silly pictures from back in the day.
Time's a juggler, dropping memories, oh!
I slip on a banana peel, and off I go.

Worms in tuxedos, are playing charades,
While time spins around, making wild escapades.
Each twist and each turn, leads to laughter near,
As I trip on the memories I hold so dear.

The Clutch of Nostalgia

Potato chips and soda pop,
We thought we'd never stop.
We laughed till our bellies shook,
The secret's in that silly book.

Tangled hair and mismatched socks,
Wishing time would stop its clocks.
In the attic, treasures piled high,
Yet all we found were some old ties.

Jumping through the wild and free,
We'd pretend we had a spree.
Now we giggle, what a twist,
But back then, we were pure bliss!

With every laugh, a tale to tell,
In our hearts, they still dwell.
A fragile moment, yet so grand,
Forever trapped in memory's hand.

Bound by Fleeting Glimpses

A sandwich made of dreams and jam,
Unruly cats just gave a damn.
We chased the sun through fields of gold,
Oh, where's the youth that we once sold?

Dancing shoes on muddy ground,
The best mistakes are always found.
Missing socks and scattered toys,
Our laughter still sings like little boys.

Sent postcards to a time long past,
"Wish you were here," we wrote so fast.
But time, the trickster, laughs away,
And still, we cherish our play.

With every glance, a smile comes near,
Echoes of joy, ringing clear.
Our moments glide on laughter's wings,
As nostalgia's tune forever sings.

Residue of Longing Dreams

Leftover cake on a paper plate,
We danced around an open gate.
Invisible friends helped us play,
While we made monsters out of clay.

The fridge adorned with silly art,
Every doodle held a part.
Sticky notes with hidden charms,
Remembering hugs and bright alarms.

Tangled tales of far-off lands,
Planets painted by small hands.
We roamed the world, but now we find,
Those memories are sweetly unkind.

Collecting echoes of laughter's zest,
In a box where time can rest.
A sprinkle of joy, a pinch of fame,
In the book of life, we write our name.

The Spectrum of Yesterday's Light

Sunshine dances upon our cheeks,
In a world where giggle speaks.
Rainbow slides and candy dreams,
Even trouble burst at the seams.

Silly hats and mismatched shoes,
Every moment, a chance to lose.
We stitched our stories with bright thread,
And now they skip, like kids, ahead.

A treasure map to laughter's door,
We rush along, seeking more.
Our heartbeats echo as we play,
While yesterday giggles at today.

In the breeze of all we remember,
We find the light, a glowing ember.
Every moment, both wild and bright,
Colors the canvas of life's delight.

Tethered by Emotion

I tripped on a thought that I had last week,
My brain, it would giggle, oh what a sneak!
Where did I leave that sandwich I made?
Tethered to laughter, my memory played.

A squirrel ran past with a nut in its mouth,
In my mind, he wore slippers, I just had to shout!
The things that I ponder, so silly and light,
Old stories revive, making everything bright.

The Veins of Remembrance

In the veins of my thoughts, old stories flow,
Like a fruitcake from Grandma—so bright and aglow!
I remember her dance moves, a sight most absurd,
She twirls through my mind, like a hummingbird.

The hat that I wore to a party so wild,
Was green with a feather, oh so fashion-challenged!
Yet here in the thicket of quirks and of quirks,
I'm laughing at missteps like comic book jerks.

The Imprint of Dreams

In my dreams, I can fly, with socks on my feet,
Where pizza grows trees, oh, isn't that neat?
A parade of lost socks, they dance in the breeze,
Singing goofy tunes while I giggle with ease.

Each dream leaves a mark, like ink on my hands,
Like a shopping list written in magical sands!
I wake up and wonder, where'd that dream go?
The imprint remains, like a musical show.

A Collage of Moments

A collage of moments, both goofy and grand,
Like the time I got stuck in a beach chair's strand.
With a bucket of ice cream, it was truly divine,
Until seagulls conspired to ruin my dine.

At a wedding, I danced like a chicken on stilts,
And they dubbed me the king of the cringe-worthy shrills.

Yet every mishap is a part of the fun,
Making memories sparkle like dew in the sun.

Reverberations of the Heart

I lost my keys, but found my shoe,
A sock is missing, is it you?
My brain's a circus, clowns on parade,
A jumbled mix, a grand charade.

I tried to cook, set off alarms,
The smoke alarm just loves my charms.
Forgot the recipe, added candy,
Dinner's a joke, but oh so dandy!

A friend once said, "Don't lose your hat!"
But where it went, I can't chat.
We laugh at what we cannot find,
The quirks of life, oh so unkind.

In all this mess, we find the cheer,
For laughter echoes, loud and clear.
With every slip and every fall,
We dance through life, through it all.

Unseen Bonds of the Past

I tripped on memories, fell in a pile,
A mix of good and awkward style.
The cat looks guilty, did you see?
He swears he's innocent, it's not he!

Old photos surface, hairdos no doubt,
Those fashion choices, what's that about?
We wore bell-bottoms, and colors so bright,
Now they haunt us, but bring delight.

At family dinners, there's tales that spin,
Grandma's wild stories always win.
"Who borrowed my sweater?" I'm quick to ask,
Yet I find it draped on the dog—what a task!

We stumble through life, with joyously wed,
In every hiccup, laughter's our thread.
With bonds unseen, that twist and bend,
We find humor in every trend.

Reflections in Still Water

Ripples dance on the pond's face,
I recall a funny duck's race.
Wobbling like a wobbly cake,
Lost in thoughts that make me quake.

The frog beside me starts to croak,
Singing tunes that make me choke.
Was that a prince I just ignored?
Or just a pal of mine, restored?

A breeze comes by, tickling my cheek,
Oh, how these memories peak!
I laugh at mishaps from long ago,
Like when I slipped in the mud and glow!

The water's calm, yet I find glee,
In all these tales that live in me.
With every splash, a giggle flows,
In this still water where laughter grows.

Sagas of the Unseen

In shadows deep, the stories hide,
Of socks that vanished, I can't abide.
Was it the dog or the sneaky cat?
Both claim innocence, how about that!

I search the drawers, I search the floor,
Finding treasures I can't ignore.
A rubber chicken, a broken toy,
Each brings laughter, a moment of joy.

Ghosts of pranks that never were,
Whispering jokes like a playful blur.
I chuckle at mishaps gone awry,
Like when I taught my parrot to fly!

With each unseen tale I behold,
Life's more amusing as it unfolds.
We giggle at our mishaps so grand,
In every saga, a jest is planned.

The Weight of Echoed Smiles

A photograph falls from the wall,
Capturing laughter, a jest for all.
Smiles echo from long-ago nights,
Where tickles and giggles took flight.

At a party, a face turns red,
After a toast that went to his head.
"Who threw the cake?" the crowd would scream,
As frosting flew, it was quite the dream!

Old jokes float in the air like dust,
In every laugh, a memory's trust.
Like the time I mistook the punch,
For a bowl of soup, I had a hunch!

Now I grin, and the weight feels light,
As echoes of laughter dance in the night.
Every smile, a treasure I keep,
In this merry tapestry, laughter runs deep.

The Pulse of Recollection

In the pulse of time, funny things thrive,
Like cousin Fred's dance that's hardly alive.
Each move a mystery, or maybe a crime,
We laughed 'til we dropped, oh, what a time!

A birthday party, balloons in the air,
One popped loudly—oh the scare!
Everyone jumped, then burst into cheer,
Making that moment the highlight of the year.

In every tick of the clock's sweet sound,
Are tales of mishaps all around.
Like that trip to the zoo with a hat on my cat,
Who wore it proudly, now how 'bout that!

So take a moment, let laughter spring,
With every recollection, let joy take wing.
For in these beats, let chuckles reveal,
The pulse of the past is a delightful meal.

Hollow Lullabies

In shadows where echoes softly play,
Whispers of laughter seem to sway.
Socks from the past, they dance and twirl,
Tickling old dreams in a cotton swirl.

Jell-O once jiggled, now it just sits,
Dancing with dust, throwing fits.
Grandma's old chair creaks with glee,
As memories spill like spilled tea.

Marbles of burden roll down the street,
Through sidewalk cracks, they find their beat.
Each bounce a giggle, each crash a grin,
Life's little jokes wrapped in a spin.

So let's toast to wrinkles from youthful glee,
To funny quirks we all decree.
Riding the waves of what once was grand,
Funny how memories stick like sand.

Fading Footsteps

Shoes left behind, they tell a tale,
Of silly races that seemed to fail.
Every scuff a story, every smudge a laugh,
Chasing shadows in a silly craft.

Footprints at dusk, a messy affair,
Glittery giggles float in the air.
Wobbly strolls on a bright Sunday,
Fading fast like a limited play.

Bouncing backtracks, a comical sight,
Where did they go? It feels so light.
Over the puddles and under the sun,
Laughter leftovers, oh what fun!

With socks mispaired, they lead the way,
Each step a chuckle, come what may.
Fading echoes of silliness rise,
In every reminiscence, humor implies.

The Dance of Remembrance

A polka of pixels in a dusty haze,
Twirl in the past with a funny gaze.
Socks with holes join in the fun,
Spinning like crazy under the sun.

Battery wars with old toys, you see,
Making robot moves in rickety glee.
Each flip a chuckle, each spin a shout,
Memories dancing, there's no doubt.

Puzzles missing pieces but oh so bright,
A laugh or two makes everything right.
Shadows twist, and echoes play,
Reminding us to dance this way.

So grab your shoes and lace them tight,
Join in the dance, it feels just right.
For in the ballet of our yesterdays,
Laughter leads and joy still stays.

Unwritten Letters to the Past

A stack of letters, unopened and neat,
A comedy of errors wrapped in a sheet.
With silly doodles and smudged ink lines,
Picturing the past as a circus of signs.

Locked in a drawer with a playful sigh,
They giggle at secrets no one can buy.
Words left unspoken, like whispers in air,
Come dance on the page with nary a care.

Mistakes in grammar, oh what a sight,
Each pen stroke laughing day and night.
Pages of chaos, wild and absurd,
Imagination's flight without a word.

In quiet corners, we let them rest,
These jester's notes which we've suppressed.
For every unwritten tale holds a jest,
In the book of the past, we're all quite blessed.

Memories on a String

I pulled a thread, it led to you,
My favorite pair of socks, quite blue.
We danced around like silly fools,
With underwear wars, we broke the rules.

A photo stuck inside a shoe,
Glimmers of past, oh, what a view!
Exploding laughter round the bend,
Like sparklers in my mind, they send.

Gum on pavement where we once played,
Sticky moments that won't just fade.
The time we thought we saw a ghost,
Turns out, it was my socks we'd toast!

So here we are, with threads so bright,
Life's silly fabric gives us delight.
In every stitch, I'll find my glee,
This string of laughs, you thread with me.

The Silent Witnesses

In grandma's attic, dust bunnies stir,
With old toys giggling, they plan and confer.
A stuffed bear with one button eye,
Watches all as years drift by.

A clock that chimes with no hands at all,
Counts moments that make the best calls.
Those echoes of laughter, a tickle or two,
How did that yogurt stay fresh, who knew?

Old records spinning like crazy tops,
They still remember the fun never stops.
The awkward dance moves we tried to own,
Played back like magic on a tinfoil throne.

While we keep living, they stay unbowed,
Silent witnesses to our laughter loud.
In their stillness, memories gleam,
A whimsical parade, a daydream's dream.

Echoes Beneath the Surface

Ripples in puddles, mischief afloat,
A splash of humor, not too remote.
Frog leaps by, wearing a crown,
To catch a fly, he jumps up and down.

On windy days, the kites collide,
When squirrels decide to take a ride.
A voice from beneath the waves does laugh,
"Who knew trees could create such a gaffe?"

Lost keys talking in the dark of night,
Sighing tales of days gone light.
The fridge hums secrets of last week's feast,
While leftovers wiggle, craving a beast!

The gurgles and giggles from shallow creeks,
Underneath the surface, the funny speaks.
If memories could swim, oh, what a race,
With laughter as bubbles all over the place!

The Ties That Bind

Two shoelaces tangled in a knot,
A pair of best friends, so tied up on the spot.
They joke about running marathons,
And end up sitting, wearing silly pons.

A belt that sings when the waistline grows,
Unforgiving, it plays up on woes.
But with every laugh, we tighten them more,
Belly laughs help us never to score!

Friendship bracelets made with glue,
Colorful memories, sticky and true.
They strangle us lovingly, hold on so tight,
Through midnight snacks and pancake fights.

Ties of life, silly threads that bind,
In the laughter, what joy we find.
Together we wander, with ties unwind,
In the quilt of our stories, forever entwined.

The Heart's Archive

In a box of odd old socks,
I found a note that says, 'Don't knock!'
A rubber chicken and a hat,
Memories, oh where they're at!

A dance with spuds, that blushing smile,
A mishap left a lasting style.
The ice cream spill on Auntie Sue,
Now every cone's a game of 'who knew?'

My childhood bike with wobbly wheels,
Thinks it's a car, oh how it squeals.
Each scrape and bruise, a story to tell,
Of pop-tart breakfasts that never went well.

An old cassette with tunes so right,
Played backwards in the middle of the night.
Laughter echoes, the heart's delight,
Old memories still make me feel light.

Flickers of the Past

An old film reel spins with flair,
Fuzzy images floating in air.
A cat in shades, a dog on a board,
It's funny how laughter's restored.

Balloons that drifted up to the sky,
With wishes that flew, oh my, oh my!
A paper plane made from last week's news,
Takes me back to childhood blues.

A mishmash of crayons, bright and bold,
Every scribble a story untold.
The fridge door served as an art display,
Mom's ear-piercing scream saved the day!

Ghosts of pizza parties sublime,
Sticky fingers, cheers in good time.
Bouncing memories like popcorn in a pan,
Flickers of joy - oh, isn't it grand?

Resonance of Familiar Places

The treehouse whispers, 'Come and play!'
With squeaky swings that sway all day.
Wobbly steps to the zip line's thrill,
Where laughter rings across the hill.

The corner store with candy galore,
Tales of mischief, just wanting more.
Gumballs decorated with sticky grace,
Each flavor a memory in that space.

The old playground, the slide so steep,
Laughing toddlers in a heap!
Tripping over bags of dreams,
Cake faces and whipped cream themes.

The park bench where secrets are shared,
Belly laughs that show we cared.
Echoes linger in the air,
Funny stories we all can share.

The Timeless Echo

A clock chimes ten, I drink some tea,
But wait – is that a talking bee?
It buzzes tales of days gone by,
Of pies that flopped and pie in the sky.

An echoing laugh from a distant past,
Oh, how those cookie crumbs were cast!
A sock puppet show that went awry,
With misfit hats that just won't die.

Old shoes left by the front door,
Each scuff a stamp of adventures galore.
The cat walks by with a smug little grin,
Thoughts of where those shenanigans begin.

Photo albums, a wobbly stack,
With snapshots of a rubber band attack.
The timeless echo of life so cheery,
In the gallery of giggles, never weary.

Unspoken Sentiments

In a drawer lies a sock, quite shy,
Hiding tales of days gone by.
Whispers of laughter, a misshaped dance,
Still it clings on to its chance.

A pinky promise etched in dust,
Forgotten brunch, abandon, and rust.
Giggling about a spilled cup of tea,
Now a legend of you and me.

Fridge magnets, old and cracked,
Each one has a story unpacked.
Every wobbly letter sings a tune,
Even the cat's left some cartoon.

Collecting memories like silly hats,
Those sticky notes, and wiggly chats.
Life's giggles hang in the air,
Float like toasts, bobbing with flair.

Palimpsest of Feelings

Ghosts of old snacks in the cupboard,
Trace crumbs on the floor, disturb the absurd.
Lollipops lost, yet thoughts remain clear,
What flavor was that? Oh dear, oh dear!

A playlist forgotten, now plays alone,
Tunes from our youth, like a whiny drone.
Singing in cars, off-key delight,
Were we sober? Not that night!

A failed soufflé lies in the past,
With dreams of fluffy, it never did last.
Cake crumbs and jokes, a buffet of glee,
More rancid than aged brie!

In every picture, a grin turns grim,
But we laugh at the bite of a whim.
Time's jesting ticks, in this mad ballet,
Remind us to dance, come what may!

Silhouettes in the Mind

Shadows creep on a wall, quite bleak,
Are those memories? Or just a peek?
They dance on the edge of a whimsical thought,
Paint the picture of what we forgot.

Old shirts that still smell of last year's fun,
Peeking from corners where old dreams run.
The ghost of a party's last marzipan,
With laughter spilling, as only we can.

Chasing down snacks in the night's soft glow,
Who stole the chocolate? We'd like to know!
Blame it on the dog, or the fridge's sweet knell,
Which opened its depths with secrets to tell.

Time hiccups, as we quirkily trace,
Smiles bloom in this silly old space.
We're silhouettes printed on the canvas of fate,
Joking along in a whimsical state.

The Echoes of Intimacy

A calendar marked with duct tape stars,
Hiccups of plans and leap-frog wars.
Inside jokes scribbled on napkins and more,
Every laugh a memory, every knock at the door.

Silly secrets baked in the oven,
Like cookies that dare us to keep on lovin'.
The voice of a friend, sweet serenade,
Haunts the halls where joy's never delayed.

Underneath the couch, we find hidden gold,
Lost crumbs of laughter, stories retold.
Bubbles and giggles float past the clock,
Bear hugs exchanged; a delightful shock!

In echoes soft, we're wrapped like a gift,
Memories jingle, our spirits they lift.
Through tickles of time, we'll sing this tune,
Underneath the light of a quirky moon.

Echoes of Yesterday

In the cupboard, my socks have a fight,
Last worn on a rather wild night.
One claims it danced, the other just slept,
While I search for a shoe, my patience inept.

Laughing at photos of friends in a thrift,
When mullets ruled all, and fashion was a gift.
We giggle at memories, our hair in a twist,
Time reveals the laughter, how could we resist?

Running to parties, all dressed up in flair,
But unknown to us, we forgot all our hair.
The photos come back, a sight so absurd,
Who wore what, and why, was never inferred!

Old toys in a box, they dream of their day,
When we used to play, not a care in the fray.
Yet now they're just mysteries, whispers of fun,
Calling us back, for the nostalgia run.

The Weight of Forgotten Moments

I found a green shirt that once was so bright,
But now it's a relic best left out of sight.
It laughs as it hangs, a ghost from the past,
A wardrobe joke that just didn't last.

Bumping into places where we once had fun,
With wobbly tables and drinks by the ton.
Yet somehow it's all just a blur in the air,
Like trying to remember if I brushed my hair.

Oh, the times we would slip, trip, and fall,
Turning graceful moves into a slapstick brawl.
Each moment a hoot, like a circus parade,
The weight of these mishaps will never quite fade.

In this sea of giggles, I toss and I dive,
Sinking in laughter while trying to thrive.
These fragments of humor, like feathers, they float,
A boat made of memories, keeping me afloat.

Shattered Reflections

A mirror that's cracked tells a tale of old,
Of mishaps and goofs that are funny, not bold.
Each shard brings a grin to the face that it shows,
Do I have a weird pimple? Who knows! Who knows!

We'd dance in the kitchen, so silly and free,
Great moves turned to chaos—how can this be me?
With flour on our noses and laughter galore,
I'd trip on the rug and we'd tumble to the floor!

In photographs taken, I blink at just the wrong time,
Caught with my mouth full and looking quite prime.
Friends laugh like hyenas at my puzzling grimace,
As time weaves together our joy and our grace.

Though shattered reflections might hold bits of strife,
They bring back the moments that lighten our life.
Through foggy reminders, we chuckle and play,
These snippets of laughter just won't slip away.

Threads of Time Woven

I stitched together tales from each quirky chat,
Like grandma's old quilt with patches of fat.
Each square holds a story, a slip or a trip,
A sock puppet saga, a wild little blip.

In my backyard, we'd build a fort just for fun,
Where superheroes gathered, oh, how they'd run!
With capes made of sheets, and snacks piled high,
We thought we were legends, reaching the sky.

Once my dog swiped a sandwich from my plate,
It flew through the air—it was quite the fate!
A memory woven with crumbs and delight,
As we laughed till we cried on that comical night.

So let's toast to our past, to giggles and cheer,
For moments now faded but still oh-so-clear.
These threads of warm laughter, stitched bright and anew,
Remind us that joy can always break through.

The Anchored Heart

In the attic, dust bunnies play,
Old postcards dance, bright as day.
Grandma's recipes, a culinary feat,
Burnt toast memories, never quite sweet.

Sock puppets wear a vintage grin,
Spilling secrets from way back when.
A baseball glove, with stories to tell,
Closed in a box where lost things dwell.

Laughter echoes in the creaky floor,
A pet rock collection behind the door.
Old roller skates, a brave attempt,
Tangled in tales of how we slept.

A photo album that makes us roar,
With hairstyles we'd rather ignore.
Each snapshot caught in a silly pose,
Painting our lives with giggles and woes.

Weaving Threads of Yesterday

A sweater crafted with love and care,
Stitch by stitch, tales we share.
Granddad's hat from that rainy day,
Worn too proudly, come what may.

The marble collection, clinking bright,
Each one a memory, a playful sight.
Jokes spun around like a whimsy kite,
Time warps here, laughter takes flight.

A yo-yo lands with a rebellious twang,
Recalling mishaps that made us sang.
Crayons melted in a sunny spill,
Rescue rescue, yet—bring that thrill!

Each thread we weave, a tangled dance,
Crafting our stories, a loving chance.
Whimsical echoes in the fabric's weave,
In every stitch, we choose to believe.

The Archive of What Remains

In a box labeled 'Odds and Ends,'
Curios gather, like old friends.
A rubber chicken from days of yore,
Silent laughter, waiting to soar.

Cereal boxes filled with dreams,
Slip 'n slides and broken beams.
Notes exchanged with scribbles and hearts,
Reminding us life's the best of arts.

A clunky toy from a yard sale find,
Squeaks softly, overjoyed and blind.
Mismatched socks with wild, bold stripes,
Throwback stories in their grumpy types.

In this archive, no room for gloom,
Just bits of cheer in every room.
Memories linger, drawing a smile,
We measure time in laughter's style.

When Time Stood Still

On a lazy Sunday, all is well,
A clock ticks softly, no need to quell.
Pajamas worn 'til the sun goes down,
In this stillness, we wear the crown.

An old bike waits, rusting away,
Inviting adventure, come what may.
Each pedal's a chuckle from years gone by,
You crash, I laugh—oh my, oh my!

A game of marbles, the floor's a stage,
Fighting the urge to turn the page.
With each flick, we jostle and roll,
Capturing moments, pure as coal.

Then laughter floods as snacks appear,
Time's frozen; we have no fear.
With friends beside and tales to spill,
In this snapshot, the heart's fulfilled.

Threads Woven in Silence

In the attic, socks collide,
Old photos laugh, in forgotten pride.
Grandma's recipes, a sticky mess,
Flour on the cat, but we must confess.

Dust bunnies dance in a wobbly row,
Silly stories from long ago.
Like spaghetti stuck to the wall,
Memories stick, we can't recall.

A broken clock with a silly chime,
Ticking tales of youth and grime.
Under the bed, what do we find?
Leftover snacks of a different kind!

So here we are, with giggles loud,
Wrapped in a blanket, feeling proud.
In this quiet, quirky space,
The humor found in time and grace.

Traces of an Old Song

A melody hums from the dusty shelf,
Could it be me or my other self?
Singing off-key with a spoon for a mic,
Two left feet in a funny hike.

Grandpa's jokes, like smoke rings rise,
Truths tangled up in old, wise lies.
The cat hums along with a purr in tune,
As we waltz with memories beneath the moon.

Baking mishaps with flour on noses,
Giggling fits and playful poses.
Critters peek with curious eyes,
They're the judges of our loony ties.

So here we sway, in the living room,
Finding joy in a subtle bloom.
Each note a thread in our fabric spun,
With laughter and love, we have our fun!

The Web of Forgotten Dreams

In the corner lies my old balloon,
A memory grounded, singing a tune.
Spider webs sway with stories untold,
Tangled and twisted, some new, some old.

A bicycle waiting, rusting away,
Bells ringing softly, wishing to play.
Underneath the stars, we'd race and glide,
But now it's a relic, like dreams, we hide.

Old toys whisper, calling my name,
In their stillness, nothing's the same.
Tickle fights and midnight plans,
All lost in the web we've spun with hands.

Yet here we laugh, remembering back,
Each silly moment helps keep us on track.
Through giggles and joy, the heart finds its way,
In every lost dream, there's humor at play.

Footfalls Through the Years

Footprints dance on the kitchen floor,
Some lead to snacks, and maybe more.
With cookie crumbs and a fresh ice cream,
These silly steps ignite a beam.

The squeaky chair has a tale to tell,
Of days gone by, oh so swell.
Mom's favorite quotes, slightly askew,
Every echo adds laughter too.

Jumping frogs and puddles splashed,
Running from chores, oh how we hurried past.
Slippers sliding on a wooden hall,
Each stumble a story, let's recall.

So here's to our walk through the joyous maze,
Reminiscing the fun of our younger days.
With every step, we laugh and cheer,
In the footfalls of life, love draws us near.

Traces of Liminal Journeys

In the attic, dust bunnies hide,
Lost socks dance with nowhere to glide.
Old photos whisper, giggle and tease,
As I search for my long-lost keys.

The cat watches with a judgy glare,
As I trip on toys sprawled everywhere.
I stumble through joy, I trip through glee,
Perhaps memories are playing tricks on me.

A forgotten diary spills all its beans,
Of childhood crushes and silly scenes.
With a sprinkle of wit, it's quite a charmer,
Oh my, did I really think he was a farmer?

In this maze of recollection and fun,
Each corner holds laughter, each door's a pun.
Like a clown on a tricycle, wobbly and bright,
These silly escapades tickle my mind light.

The Haunting of Old Footsteps

Echoes of laughter dance down the hall,
Toys from the past are having a ball.
A ghost with a rubber chicken in hand,
Lurking in shadows, it's quite unplanned!

These dusty old shoes start to tap, tap, tap,
As I trip over thoughts, what a marvelous flap!
With each creaky floorboard, secrets reveal,
What was once serious now feels surreal.

The portraits grin wide with a knowing smirk,
As I dodge flying memories that oddly lurk.
"Did you really wear that?" one voice gently sneers,
"Shush! I'm just here for the ice cream, my dears!"

Yet through this spook fest, I cannot deny,
There's joy in the echoes that flutter and fly.
With laughter and silliness so vividly clear,
The past is a party that I hold dear!

Beyond the Veil of Time

Through time's cheeky, twisting lane,
I see all my slip-ups, oh what a strain!
My past self waves, a pancake in hand,
Flipping memories like they're part of the band.

Tall tales bounce like a rubber ball,
Of family dinners that turned into brawl.
With pie on my face and cake in my hair,
I wonder if time is truly fair!

The silly moments are stashed like confetti,
Those whims that surely keep me all sweaty.
"Remember that time?" the echoes all laugh,
While my future self just scours the staff.

Yet through visions of wobbly past escapades,
I revel in joy, let the laughter cascade.
The veil may be thin, but I wear it with pride,
For life is a parody, let's take this wild ride!

Memories in a Glass Jar

In a glass jar, peculiar things sway,
Jellybeans, giggles, and yesterday's fray.
Each candy holds stories, both sweet and bizarre,
Of unplanned adventures and the wanted bizarre.

I unscrew the lid, whiffs tickle my nose,
A scent of nostalgia, as the playfulness grows.
"Who threw the cake?" echoes loud in my head,
With voices of past, like they're just overhead.

Marbles roll 'round with mischievous cheer,
Carrying secrets of days far from sheer.
I chuckle and giggle, so reminiscent—
Were we really that silly? Oh goodness, I'm spent!

With each looking back, the bubbles arise,
Memories sparkle, like stars in the skies.
In this glass jar, I keep things in sight,
And please let them dance in the laughter-filled night!

Ghostly Whispers

In the attic I hear a voice,
Telling jokes that leave me no choice.
A laugh so loud, it flips my hat,
I'm sure it's just my old cat.

The dishes rattle, a ghostly cheer,
I ask my potted plant to hear.
It shakes its leaves, a giggle in green,
Is this a prank, or just a routine?

Bumping shadows on the wall,
Cackling echoes of the hall.
A stepladder does a little jig,
Suggesting I dance a silly dig.

In this house, old tales collide,
With every creak, my spirit's fried.
Laughing ghosts we can't decode,
Turning memories into a comedy road.

Echoed Emotions

A sock appears from nowhere at night,
Is it just me or can socks take flight?
With dance moves, they twist and they shout,
In this laundry, no room for doubt.

Last week's meal waits with a grin,
It whispers softly, 'Try me again!'
I just giggle, push it aside,
That leftover lasagna is little too wide.

The walls are plastered with laughter's paint,
Haunted by stories neither quaint.
A picture frame winks, what a sight,
Did I just eat cake? Oh, what a delight!

Happiness echoes down the lane,
Running from feelings that are insane.
Like a rubber chicken that just won't stop,
Memory's a party; let the fun drop!

Distorted Reflections

In the mirror, a clown gives a wink,
"What happened to you?" my past seems to think.
With a nose that's red and hair all wild,
The reflection laughs, oh, what a child!

Old snapshots have a funny way,
Turning gray skies into bright buffet.
With every click, a quirk in time,
Matching mugs like an old rhyme.

Funny mirrors warp my grin,
And suddenly, I'm wearing a fin.
Squinting at memories, twisted and spun,
I laugh so hard, but am I done?

These echoes dance, they prance all day,
Shaping my thoughts in a playful ballet.
Just watch out for that lady in plaid,
Her hairstyle's a memory that's also bad!

Map of the Soul's Journey

With a zigzag line and a dotted path,
I navigate life and its crazy math.
Each twist and turn gives a chuckle or two,
What's next? A llama in a tutu?

Ink spills memories, bright and absurd,
Uncharted lands, where laughters stirred.
Navigating through giggles and cheers,
Sailing on boats made of old fears.

I glance at old roads, paved with delight,
Silly detours shine brightly at night.
With compass in hand, I voyage afar,
Who knew my ticket was a candy bar?

So here's to the map, a whimsical chart,
Of laughter and love, an artful start.
In the journey of souls, we happily roam,
Finding joy in the quirks that feel like home.

Embers of Longing

In the attic, old clothes hide,
Whispers of fashion, I can't abide.
Pants so baggy, shirts with flair,
I try them on, but it's a scare.

Last summer's drink, a peachy delight,
Turns into a flop at first bite.
Memories dance, but the taste is off,
I laugh at the past, and just pop and scoff.

Photos stuck in a dusty frame,
A wedding once fancy, now feeling lame.
Uncle Joe's toupee, how it did fly,
I laugh till I snort, oh my, oh my!

Yet here I stand, gloom never near,
For quirky tales bring laughter, I cheer.
With every glance at history's bling,
I twirl around, as I break out and sing!

Paths Not Taken

I pondered a road filled with ballpoint pens,
Which turned into a writer's weekend zen.
But I chose the one where socks mismatch,
And now my life's a colorful patch.

In line for coffee, I let out a snort,
It's all beans and dreams, a messy report.
The choices I made tumble in haste,
Yet every error, I'd never waste.

Skipped the gym for a dance-off spree,
Now my moves scare the cat and the tree.
At every misstep, I chuckle and grin,
Our pasts are the jokes that keep us in spin.

So here we are, with laughter and cheer,
Those paths not taken seem perfectly clear.
I'd stumble and trip through old photographs,
Each moment a giggle, a reason to laugh!

A Portrait of Long Ago

In a frame, a picture of hair gone wild,
A style so bold, was I really a child?
The colors I wore scream louder than drums,
Yet now they bring chuckles, and silly hums.

My grandma's hugs had a scent of pies,
But her stories were taller than the skies.
Between the giggles and floury cheek,
Her tales of my dad? They were quite the freak!

That quilt on the sofa tells tales of yarn,
Of loss and of laughter, it's slightly worn.
But every stitch holds a smile, tucked tight,
In every odd corner, there's humor in sight.

So here's to the past, those whimsical days,
Where everyone trips in their own quirky ways.
We paint with the laughter that echoes so bold,
And treasure these portraits, both silly and old.

Serenade of the Familiar

In the kitchen, there's chaos and cheer,
As I boil up water, with naught but a smear.
Funny how pasta can dance in the pot,
While I'm over here chasing a spoon that is not!

The cat on the counter inspects every dish,
As I serenade him, "You really are swish!"
He pretends not to care, with a flick of his tail,
Yet his eyes gleam with mischief, a curious trail.

Old friends call up, with stories anew,
Of socks with holes and mishaps, too!
We laugh about chairs that break when they see,
The wonderful chaos of you and of me.

So raise up a glass, let's toast to the fun,
To the quirks and the trips that life has begun.
In familiar grounds where oddities dwell,
We sing out our stories, both silly and swell!

The Lament of Old Photographs

Faded smiles in sepia tones,
Whiskered cats and silly phones.
Grandpa's hair, a wild old mess,
Caught mid-dance, what a finesse!

Uncle Joe in a chicken suit,
Danced away on a trampoline's loot.
Mismatched socks and rubber bands,
Captured moments with clumsy hands.

Now they sit on dusty shelves,
Telling tales of younger selves.
When life was wild and shoes were bright,
Now we listen with delight!

Oh, the tales these photos weave,
Of missing socks and tricks up sleeves.
In every corner, laughter rings,
In every snap, absurdity sings.

Ties of Nostalgia

Remember the time we wore that hat?
A monstrosity, who thought of that?
With feathers bright and colors bold,
Our fashion sense was purest gold!

From cupcakes baked with way too much dough,
To secret clubs where no one would go.
We built a fort of sheets and chairs,
Where imagination danced without any cares.

Oh, cousin Tim with a frog on his cheek,
Claimed it was luck, but we all had a peek.
Laughter spilled like lemonade,
Moments like these are never delayed.

Through silly games and endless pranks,
We forged adventures, filled the ranks.
Ties of the past keep chuckles alive,
In our hearts, those giggles thrive.

A Tapestry of Yesteryears

Threads of laughter sewn so tight,
A tapestry spun from sheer delight.
Awkward poses, goofy grins,
Captured moments, where humor begins.

A mime in the park, a slip on the ice,
All stitched together, oh so nice.
A barbecue mishap, smoke in the air,
We learned quickly: don't forget the flare!

Old bikes with bells, all rusty and bright,
A race to the hill, oh what a sight!
With skinned knees and triumphant cheers,
This weaving of laughter spans many years.

In every thread, a story is spun,
A tapestry filled with laughter and fun.
Colors blend under joyful sunbeams,
In this quilt of past hopes and dreams.

The Veil of Remembering

Behind the veil, a teasing jest,
Who knew our pasts would be such a quest?
The cake that flopped, the dog that ran,
These memories make us who we are, man!

Laundry day many moons ago,
We sent shirts flying, oh what a show!
Popsicle sticks held a fort so grand,
Until dad tripped, and lost his stand.

A treasure hunt for lost car keys,
Led us to birds and buzzing bees.
With treasure found, we laughed till we cried,
In every mishap, joy would abide.

The veil of days past drapes just so,
Filling our hearts with a gentle glow.
Remember, as we all gather 'round,
Laughter's the treasure that always is found.

Embracing the Unseen

In my attic, ghosts play tricks,
They juggle old socks, just for kicks.
I trip over memories, what a sight,
A dance of the silly, under moonlight.

A hat from a cat I once adored,
It whispers sweet secrets, quite ignored.
Each shoe I find has a tale to tell,
Of trips to the fridge, oh what a spell!

Puppet strings made of my bedtime fears,
They chuckle as I sip my brightly colored beers.
With every lost thought, a new one appears,
I toast to the past, it cheers and jeers!

When fortune cookies sprout legs and dance,
They waltz with my cereal, quite a chance.
Yet, in this chaos, I find pure fun,
In the unseen laughter, we're all one.

Songs of Echoing Heartbeats

I sing to the shadows that follow me round,
They hum the tunes of a lost playground.
With each skip and hop, they stir and play,
Whistling forgotten songs from yesterday.

My fridge sings a song, if you catch it right,
Of lettuce' dreams in the dead of night.
While pancakes plot mischief, stacked on high,
They flip for their freedom, oh my, oh my!

In the drawer, spoons hold a secret rave,
They boogie with forks, oh so brave!
Plates join the chorus, a clatter of cheer,
As I roll my eyes, but still want to hear.

So raise a glass to the echoes in time,
With a giggle and grin, we all play sublime.
In the silly embrace of forgotten dreams,
Heartbeats dance to the giggly themes.

Whispers of the Past

Beneath the bed lies a treasure trove,
Where mismatched socks have learned to rove.
They whisper sweet nothings to dust bunnies,
Trading tales of socks friends from old punny counties.

A record player spins 'round with glee,
Playing tunes that laugh at me.
With each scratch and pop, I'm taken back,
To dance parties in pajamas, what a knack!

Old photos wink with a knowing grin,
At hairdos so bold, they'd never win.
And grandpa's mustache that made him a star,
Still tickles my memory, oh my, how bizarre!

With echoes of laughter, we share the scene,
In a world where the silly reigns supreme.
The past isn't heavy; it's a playful tease,
Whispering joy in the autumn breeze.

Echoes in the Silence

In the quiet, I hear a faint yawn,
As pillows conspire from dusk till dawn.
They shuffle around with dreams untold,
Plotting to tickle me, brazen and bold.

A teapot chuckles, with steam as its voice,
Whispering secrets, oh what a choice!
Each cup has a story, froth in the air,
Of stupid bets and backyard fair.

In the corners, shadows exchange shy winks,
Trading old pranks like wise little links.
They nudge the cat, with a flick of a tail,
She jumps, then pouts, oh what a fail!

So here's to the moments lost in the fun,
Where echoes of laughter will never be done.
In silence, we revel, like kids full of glee,
With whispers of nonsense, eternally free.

The Weight of Recollection

I forgot my keys, they were right here,
But they hid themselves, oh dear!
Pants on my head, quite the sight,
Searching for memories, day and night.

The cat stole my lunch, what a sneaky thief,
Dancing around like a furry chief.
Lost in thought, and then I tripped,
Banana peels make my ego flipped.

Old photos emerge, my hair was a mess,
What was I thinking? I must confess.
Trying to recall just what we said,
But all I find is a picture of bread.

When laughter echoes from long ago,
Every mishap is ensuring the show.
As I sift through the foggy past,
I wonder how long these giggles will last.

Shadows in the Attic

Dust bunnies tango with my old shoes,
A party of shadows, I can't refuse.
Faded whispers of yesteryears,
Dance in the dark, coaxing out cheers.

I found my old bike, but where is the rust?
A time machine's missing, in it I trust.
Grandma's old stories, they tumble and spin,
How did I think I was good at the violin?

An old clock ticks, but what time is it now?
Two minutes to chaos, I solemnly vow.
Boxes of memories, they giggle and squeak,
Their secrets, I listen, week after week.

In the attic, those shadows won't quit,
They bounce with old jokes, a comedic skit.
Through the cobwebs of laughter, I roam,
Each shadow's a jest, a memory's home.

Bound by the Echoes

Each echo of laughter, a riddle I hear,
A chorus of friends from yesteryear.
Tripping on thoughts from delightful nights,
Endless giggles turn to playful flights.

In the backyard, we spun like a top,
Until someone fell, and we couldn't stop.
The ghosts of our pranks still linger around,
Chasing the echoes, our old joyful sound.

As I sift through old boxes, what do I find?
A sock puppet that appears out of line.
In the mirror of time, I glimpse my old self,
Worn-out memories stacked on the shelf.

They taunt me with tales of snacks we consumed,
I chase down the past, oh how we bloomed.
A party of echoes and stories entwined,
In the shadow of laughter, we're still unconfined.

Fragments of What Once Was

In a corner, a puzzle, pieces amiss,
A jumble of fragments, a nostalgic bliss.
Did we eat all the cookies or just one?
The crumbs tell me tales of past silly fun.

Flashbacks arrive with a slip and a slide,
A paper airplane, we took for a ride.
Our faces were bright, swung wild in the breeze,
Until we collided, both down on our knees.

A balloon from a party, all limp and forlorn,
Reminds me of laughter until the next morn.
As I bend down to pick up a stray toy,
I burst into giggles, oh what a ploy!

The fragments are key, each bit holds a jest,
In the scrapbook of life, we form our own fest.
Recalling the laughter, in moments like this,
Each piece is a memory wrapped up in bliss.

www.ingramcontent.com/pod-product-compliance
Lightning Source LLC
Chambersburg PA
CBHW060143230426
43661CB00003B/550